Remembering
Toledo

Gregory M. Miller

TRADE PAPER
PRESS

The passengers on this train rolling across the New York Central Bridge about 1896 would have an excellent view of the developing skyline of Toledo. Church spires still predominated before the turn of the century, but the era of the skyscraper would emerge during the next decade. The structure near the center of the bridge that looks like a ship is actually the mechanism that pivoted the bridge to allow ships to pass through.

Remembering
Toledo

Turner Publishing Company
200 4th Avenue North • Suite 950
Nashville, Tennessee 37219
(615) 255-2665

Remembering Toledo

www.turnerpublishing.com

Library of Congress Control Number: 2010924252

ISBN: 978-1-59652-642-6

Printed in the United States of America

10 11 12 13 14 15 16—0 9 8 7 6 5 4 3 2 1

CONTENTS

This aerial view features both sides of the river, with a busy Toledo Marine Terminal at center-left. The opening of the St. Lawrence Seaway in 1959 provided a short boom in Great Lakes shipping, but by the mid-1970s the Marine Terminal had closed (it has since been reborn as the Docks).

Acknowledgments

This volume, *Remembering Toledo,* would not have been possible without the diligent efforts, over many years, of the dedicated staff and volunteers at the Onondaga Historical Association. Past OHA director Richard N. Wright's work with the photography collection should be especially noted and the current assistance of archivist Michael Flanagan is greatly appreciated.

PREFACE

Toledo has thousands of historic photographs that reside in archives, both locally and nationally. This book began with the observation that, while those photographs are of great interest to many, they are not easily accessible. During a time when Toledo is looking ahead and evaluating its future course, many people are asking, How do we treat the past? These decisions affect every aspect of the city—architecture, public spaces, commerce, infrastructure—and these, in turn, affect the way that people live their lives. This book seeks to provide easy access to a valuable, objective look into the history of Toledo.

The power of photographs is that they are less subjective than words in their treatment of history. Although the photographer can make subjective decisions regarding subject matter and how to capture and present it, photographs seldom interpret the past to the extent textual histories can. For this reason, photography is uniquely positioned to offer an original, untainted look at the past, allowing the viewer to learn for himself what the world was like a century or more ago.

This project represents countless hours of review and research. The researchers and writer have reviewed thousands of photographs in numerous archives. We greatly appreciate the generous assistance of the individuals and organizations listed in the acknowledgments of this work, without whom this project could not have been completed.

The goal in publishing this work is to provide broader access to this set of extraordinary photographs that seek to inspire, provide perspective, and evoke insight that might assist people who are responsible for determining Toledo's future. In addition, the book seeks to preserve the past with adequate respect and reverence.

With the exception of touching up imperfections that have accrued with the passage of time and cropping where necessary, no changes have been made. The focus and clarity of many images are limited to the technology and the ability of the photographer at the time they were recorded.

The work is divided into eras. Beginning with some of the earliest known photographs of Toledo, the first section records photographs through the end of the nineteenth century. The second section spans the beginning of the twentieth century up to the eve of the Great Depression. Section Three moves from the depression to World War II and the years immediately following. The last section covers the postwar decades to 1975.

In each of these sections we have made an effort to capture various aspects of life through our selection of photographs. People, commerce, transportation, infrastructure, religious institutions, and educational institutions have been included to provide a broad perspective.

We encourage readers to reflect as they go walking in Toledo, strolling through the city, its parks, and its neighborhoods. It is the publisher's hope that in utilizing this work, longtime residents will learn something new and that new residents will gain a perspective on where Toledo has been, so that each can contribute to its future.

—Todd Bottorff, Publisher

By 1872, the Western Manufacturing Company produced sashes, doors, and blinds for use in the houses that were being built in the Midwest. The standardization of these building components, combined with the new "balloon frame" method of construction, made possible the lower prices for housing that followed, which enabled working families to acquire their own home.

THE FUTURE GREAT CITY OF THE WORLD

(1870s–1899)

This is Superior Street near the corner of Adams Street, around 1877. The congregation of St. Paul Methodist-Episcopal, shown at center, later built a church on Madison Avenue. Superior and Adams streets are today at the heart of downtown, which has not seen single family dwellings for upwards of a hundred years. In 1877, however, Toledo was a walking city—most destinations could be reached by foot.

Like much of the rest of the nation, after the Civil War Toledo attempted to attract manufacturing concerns. In 1878, the city succeeded in attracting the Milburn Wagon Works to Auburndale, a newly established suburb, partly financing the construction of a factory. By the mid-1880s, Milburn claimed to be the largest wagon manufacturer in the world. This success, and the discovery of natural gas near Findlay, encouraged a second manufacturing company, the New England Glass Company, to relocate to Toledo in 1888.

Ice gorges not only damaged bridges in 1883, they also backed up water in sufficient quantity to flood downtown—especially along Water Street. The number of bridges crossing the Maumee during this earlier time created more places for ice floes to jam against, causing the river to back up. Today, because of the flatness of the landscape in Toledo and northwest Ohio, the Maumee rarely floods in Toledo proper—flooding takes place farther upriver.

The sixth-grade class at Franklin School in 1887 poses for the photographer. Franklin was located in East Toledo, on Elm between 3rd and 4th streets. By 1887, Toledo had a number of grammar schools, as well as a high school, constructed in 1853. Besides the public school system, Toledo's growing Roman Catholic population also supported grammar schools at many of the parishes that had been established.

Summit Street near Jefferson Avenue (ca. 1890). While this street cleaner is taking a cigarette break, others are busy shopping in the heart of the commercial district. Given the difficulty of preserving food before the advent of the refrigerator, food shopping was often a daily errand.

Rush hour, circa 1890, at the intersection of Cherry, Summit, and St. Clair streets. In the distance is the Cherry Street Bridge, gateway to East Toledo.

These men are members of the baseball team sponsored by the Toledo State Hospital. The team was city champion in 1894. Team sports like baseball and football were seen as a way to promote camaraderie among workers.

The Fort Industry Block, at the corner of Summit and Monroe streets (ca. 1890). The building was so named because it was thought to occupy the site of an earlier-day fort when it was first built in 1843.

The Wild West show became a staple of circuses during the 1890s, as this parade down Summit Street demonstrates. As the Western frontier shrank into oblivion, Indians became a part of the "exotic" that circus customers expected to see.

These women are taking care of the paperwork in the family business, the Lamson and Skinner Bending Company, in 1892. Lamson and Skinner specialized in bending wood for making wagon wheels.

Construction of the new Sheriff's Residence, County Jail, and Powerhouse was accompanied by the construction of a new county courthouse as well. Numerous building projects under way at the same time suggests that residents of Toledo were confident of continuing prosperity in these years.

The Lake Shore and Michigan locomotive at right is pulling through Union Station, probably on its way to the Airline Junction (ca. 1896). Toledo has long been an important rail center.

The Hartford Block was located on the southwest corner of Madison Avenue and Summit Street in 1890. The limited technology of early photography often left numerous "ghosts" in the image, as seen here.

Out with the old, in with the new. This photograph from late 1897 shows the building that served as the county courthouse from 1853 to 1897 (in the foreground) and its replacement (in the background). The larger structure was erected to accommodate the number of courtrooms needed for a growing county.

The Elk's Carnival in 1898 was a fundraiser for the organization, with proceeds going toward the purchase of property on Michigan Street that became known as "Fraternity Row."

This photograph depicts the Ohio National Guard mobilizing in 1898 to travel to Cuba as part of the Spanish-American War. Industrial unrest in the years between 1877 and 1894 spurred the construction of fortresses like this one around the nation. The Lucas County Armory was built in 1894 and was destroyed by fire in 1934—after housing Ohio National Guard troops brought in to quell the Auto-Lite strike that year.

Summit Street bustles with Christmas shoppers and traffic around the turn of the century. Many of the then-independent streetcar lines had transfer points on Summit—which was the most popular shopping destination in Toledo at the time.

From Port Town to Factory Town

(1900–1929)

Another popular means of transportation at the turn of the century was the bicycle—even by well-dressed young women like this one. The bicycle this woman is riding could well have been manufactured in Toledo—the city styled itself the "Coventry of America" (Coventry was the main bicycle manufacturing center in Great Britain), and was home to several bicycle manufacturers, as well as makers of bicycle parts.

Among the advertising campaigns boosting Toledo, this sign proclaiming "You will do better in Toledo" was one of the most dramatic. This lighted sign, together with similar displays depicting a lake freighter and a railroad engine, sat atop a building at the corner of Summit, Cherry, and St. Clair streets.

This photograph shows the comfort station at City Park, with a matron seated outside, and a park worker leaning against the building. It is part of a series of photographs that appear to have been taken at City Park around the same time. City Park, once known as Lenk's Park, was one of the oldest parks in Toledo, and this comfort station was probably part of an effort to upgrade park facilities.

This pool was located in City Park. Municipal pools were built in several city parks in the 1910s. Although there were earlier parks in Toledo, they were privately run. In the administration of Samuel M. "Golden Rule" Jones, a push was begun by Jones's associate Sylvanus Jermain to build a number of new parks, and to link them together with a boulevard system of streets. This photograph was probably made around 1914—evidence suggests that the swimming pools were added around that time.

This scene was recorded at City Park. The earliest playground in the city was in a park located at the corner of Smith and Canton streets. After observing the success of this playground in keeping children from playing in the streets, playgrounds were added to other parks. This image was probably recorded to illustrate how nicely the children were using the new equipment.

This hotel lobby displays all the amenities expected by patrons of such a space—a shoeblack, a tobacco counter, spittoons, and a comfortable place to enjoy the tobacco product.

Somewhere in this throng of people is Theodore Roosevelt, who would replace William McKinley as president in 1901 following McKinley's assassination in Buffalo.

Inspired by the popularity of the Midway at the World's Columbian Exposition of 1892-93 in Chicago, the "exotic" became a regular attraction at circuses.

John Robinson's Circus provided a three-ring show under the big top, as well as two stage shows, like this one.

The *City of Toledo* made daily excursions between Toledo and Put-in-Bay during summer months. Here the boat is just getting under way, backing away from the dock on the Maumee River. Ohio's Lake Erie Islands were a destination for citizens who could afford a second home there or hotel fare.

Aviator Roy Knabenshue won a $500 award from A. L. Spitzer for being the first dirigible pilot to land and take off from the top of the Spitzer Building in downtown Toledo. On June 30, 1905, Knabenshue piloted the *Toledo I* from the fairgrounds located at Dorr Street and Upton Avenue to the Spitzer Building, and back, in just around 30 minutes. Despite his derring-do, and the short life span of many aviators of the time, Knabenshue lived to the ripe old age of 83, dying in California in 1960—of natural causes.

Conant Street in Maumee. The welcome signs are for the Grand Army of the Republic encampment taking place downriver in Toledo, circa 1908.

A popular way for church and civic groups to raise money just after the turn of the century was to hold a "lawn fete." Front yards were usually festooned with American flags and Japanese lanterns, and guests were served light snacks and lemonade.

The lobby in the Boody House hotel around the beginning of the twentieth century. Many hotels catered to traveling salesmen, which explains the absence of women in photographs like this one.

The National Union Building was constructed by a fraternal insurance company. These companies provided working-class people with the means to afford a funeral should something untoward happen. When this building was erected in 1892, it was the tallest in Toledo; by the following year, it had lost that distinction to the Nasby Building.

The Nicholas Building site at the corner of Madison Avenue and Huron Street. The workers in view are part of a demolition crew (ca. 1905).

Washington Street. Washington has traditionally divided downtown from the Warehouse District—although just after the turn of the century, this difference was not quite so stark as it is today.

The influence of Chicago architects—particularly Louis Sullivan—is visible all around early-twentieth-century Toledo. Neither eight-story building here is tall enough to qualify as a "skyscraper," but their lack of ornamentation except at the cornice is Sullivanesque.

The amusement park at Walbridge Park was an extremely popular recreation spot for Toledoans—and would be until fire destroyed the park in 1960. This section was known as "the midway," after the Midway of the World's Columbian Exposition in Chicago, which had taken place 12 years before this 1905 photograph was made.

Lake Erie Park and Casino was located at the end of the trolley car line in point place, popular for its roller coaster and its boardwalk around the turn of the century.

Grand Army of the Republic week, in downtown Toledo, 1908. Much of the city was decorated for the event. This encampment seemed to resonate with the participants and observers, who must have recognized that there would not be many more such occasions—the Civil War had ended more than 40 years before.

This show of patriotic zeal was probably decoration for a festive Independence Day celebration circa 1912.

The Wamba Festival was held to demonstrate what a fun city Toledo could be. City leaders appropriated a mythical figure from the history of Toledo, Spain, and built a festival—with parades and the crowning of a king and queen—around it. The festival was held in 1909.

Madison Avenue, facing west from St. Clair Street, circa 1915. Madison has long been the heart of the financial district in Toledo.

Jess Willard was known as "the Great White Hope," a reference to white boxers who attempted to defeat black boxer Jack Johnson. After becoming the lone successful great white hope, defeating Johnson in Havana, Cuba, Willard refused to fight any black challengers. When Jack Dempsey became champion, he followed suit—leaving potential African-American challengers like sparring partner Robert Buckley, the "Jamaica Kid," out in the cold.

The Ohio Dairy was located near downtown, on Erie Street.

The LaSalle and Koch Department Store was located at the corner of Jefferson and Superior in 1910. Within a few years, the store moved to its new location on Adams at Huron.

The Willys-Overland Company, like many other companies of the day, often sponsored cultural activities for employees, like this concert in the engineering department in 1912.

As the center of legal activity for the county, the Lucas County Courthouse has been a busy place—especially around 1910, when this image was recorded.

Fred J. Edler was able to show off his skills as an upholsterer in his modified runabout (ca. 1910).

In view here are John and Fred Zurfluh in 1913. Their jewelry shop was on Monroe Street.

The Holmes Snowflake Laundry Building was the first Toledo location for the Champion Spark Plug Company, attracted to the city by the Willys Overland Company. Willys agreed to buy spark plugs from Robert and Frank Stranahan, if they would relocate their company to Toledo (ca. 1910).

The circus parade from the train station to the circus grounds was always a reliable way to attract a crowd, like this one circa 1910.

The Second National Bank (later Toledo Trust) building was the tallest building in Toledo when it opened in 1913. The Ohio Building surpassed it in 1930.

With airports still far and few between in 1912, pilots were always looking for new places to take off and land, sometimes on the water.

These gentlemen are looking over the cannon aboard the replica *Niagara* during the Perry Centennial in 1913.

The Perry Centennial attracted a sizable crowd to the waterfront in 1913.

This trained bear was photographed behind the old Main Library, which was located at the corner of Madison Avenue and Ontario Street. The photograph was taken about 1915.

Members of an early Scott High School track team get into position for a footrace. The school opened in 1914.

The Niagara Hotel Fire began around midnight on April 4, 1915. Two guests were killed, and several others suffered serious injuries.

Fire fighters face difficult circumstances in performing their duties, particularly when the weather turns cold. Shown here is the aftermath of the fire at Wilmington and Company about 1915.

The automobiles in this showroom were both made in Toledo, produced by the Willys-Overland Company (ca. 1915).

The swing bridge of the Wheeling and Lake Erie railroads pivoted open to allow the *Wolverine* and the *Niagara* replica to pass through—which also permitted a throng of people to get a close view of the two ships in 1913.

This is part of the crowd that went down to the Ann Arbor train station to greet the soldiers returning from World War I in 1919.

Adams Street and St. Clair Street (ca. 1919). The billboard on top of the building at center-left proclaims that "Budweiser spells Temperance."

The Vita Temple theater was home to the First Congregational church from 1878 to 1913, when the congregation moved to Collingwood Boulevard. The Temple, located on St. Clair, shared the street with a number of other theaters during the Roaring Twenties (ca. 1920).

The Knights of Columbus march down Madison Avenue, probably after ceremonies marking the opening of the Catholic Club in 1929.

Shown here is some of the destruction from the Palm Sunday tornado of 1920, which nearly blew Raab's Corners off the map.

The Secor Hotel as it appeared around the time of its opening in 1908. Unlike many other buildings of this era, this one is still in use.

The Niagara Hotel Fire drew a large crowd of spectators in April 1915.

By the 1920s, the best days of the Boody House were long gone. As the decade ended, it would be leveled to make way for the Ohio Savings Bank Building (later headquarters for Owens-Illinois).

Union Station opened in 1886, and served rail passengers well for many years. In 1950, a new station was built and the older building was demolished.

After fire damaged much of the 1886 Union Station, repairs were inadequate. Clamors for a new station finally prevailed 20 years later. The Central Union Terminal opened in 1950.

The 1920s saw the flowering of Toledo's love affair with high school football, in evidence here as a large crowd attends a game at Scott High School's Siebart Stadium in 1926.

In view here are some of the airplanes and people present for the opening of Transcontinental Airport in May 1928.

Activities were planned for all ages at the opening of Transcontinental Airport in 1929, including this group of balsa wood airplane hobbyists.

The early 1920s were a prosperous time for Toledo, and the city began building municipal structures, like the Safety Building here in 1923.

Young Jules Vinnedge helps his grandfather Julius Lamson break ground for the new downtown Lamson's department store on April 11, 1928.

St. Patrick's Roman Catholic Church has commanded the high point near downtown since 1893, when it replaced the wood-frame church that was built in 1862.

Charles Lindbergh is shown here in 1928 making an unscheduled fuel stop in Bono—the extreme eastern edge of Lucas County.

The Toledo Blade opened a new building in 1927, with President Calvin Coolidge doing the honors of turning on the electricity for the presses.

The new Lamson's Department Store was able to open its doors in time for the Christmas shopping season, November 12, 1928—after not breaking ground until April 11 of that year.

The clutter of signage and traffic on Summit Street gives no clue to the fact that Toledo—like the rest of the nation—was entering the most severe economic depression in American history (ca. 1931).

Depression and War

(1930–1949)

By 1930, the Valentine Theatre was showing movies, and touting itself as a place to come in and beat the summer heat.

The Police and Fire Alarm Building, completed in 1934, was part of the municipal building program—and one of the few examples in Toledo of the Western Reserve style of architecture.

With the worst years of the Great Depression in progress, these women walk the picket line during the Auto-Lite Strike in 1934.

Despite the slowing of economic activity during the Great Depression, the city remained an important port—particularly for the shipment of southern Ohio coal.

A young Ohio National Guardsman, suffering an injury to the head in the Battle of Chestnut Hill, is carried to safety.

Because the favorable currents of the Maumee mean there is less need for dredging, East Toledo has long been the favored area for ports.

These men are working the pots in the Libbey-Owens-Ford plant in Rossford.

During the Great Depression, the federal government under President Roosevelt threw unprecedented amounts of the public's money into economic relief programs. Boy Scouts in Lucas County benefited from federal Works Progress Administration projects, like these treehouses at Camp Miakonda.

One WPA legacy was built on Michigan Street, between Adams and Madison—the Toledo Public Library, here shown under construction in 1939.

This Neoclassical building looks like a bank—and it is. The former home of the First National Bank, it became a branch for the Toledo Trust in the 1930s.

This APCOA parking garage was located behind the Secor Hotel on Superior Street, and had the advantage of looking nothing like a parking garage—considered a mark of distinction when this photograph was taken in 1937.

The Great Ziegfeld was released in 1936. The Palace Theatre was located on St. Clair Street, along with a number of other movie theaters. Downtown at this time was *the* place to see first-run movies.

The Wheeling and Lake Erie (successor to the Ann Arbor) Railroad passenger station, as it looked circa 1940.

The Hotel Waldorf was located on Summit Street, at the corner of Jefferson Avenue, until it was demolished in 1965.

These boys under the train shed roof enjoy an excellent view of President Roosevelt.

On Summit Street, hats are 88 cents "while they last" (ca. 1940).

To sell war bonds during the Second World War, Marlene Dietrich made Toledo one of many stops on her agenda.
She is accompanied by a naval officer at the intersection of Erie and Adams Street (1942).

This streetcar ran on the Cherry Street line. It is shown here pulling past St. Francis church, preparing to turn onto Cherry (ca. 1940).

It's not the Great White Way, but Toledoans of a certain age remember that St. Clair Street downtown was home to a large number of movie houses, as well as specialty shops like Nichols Men's Wear.

Main Street in suburban Sylvania, November 1941. Sylvania sits atop an enormous deposit of Devonian age limestone, but for most of its history it remained a sleepy crossroads hamlet. In the postwar era, that image changed—Sylvania became one of the most rapidly growing municipalities in Lucas County.

The Willys-Overland Jeep was not the only contribution to the war effort that industries in Toledo made. Here a technician checks results from a wind tunnel test utilizing Toledo scales.

Jeeps are loaded onto a trailer for shipment (ca. 1941). The Jeep remained the transportation vehicle of choice in the U.S. military for more than 40 years, until introduction of the Humvee in 1985.

This photograph was taken from the 22nd floor of the Toledo Trust (Second National Bank) Building in November 1944, looking northwesterly along the Maumee River. The unknown lake freighter is headed downstream to Maumee Bay, and has cleared three of the six drawbridges operating in the 1940s on the navigable stretch of the river.

This Ice Follies skater jumped this jeep at the Icehouse, which was located near the Babcock Dairy and the Willys-Overland plant in West Toledo. The Ice Follies troupe was founded in 1937 and was featured in the movie *Ice Follies* in 1939. After the Sports Arena opened in 1948, the Icehouse found it difficult to book acts.

Tiedtke's Department Store provided customers a wide variety of products—everything from meat to moccasins—at low prices. The same idea that Sam Walton later turned into billions. The Tiedtkes, and the Kobachers after the Tiedtkes sold the store, were masters of in-store marketing. In the 1950s, bananas were not a regular grocery item—except at Tiedtke's.

THE POSTWAR DECADES

(1950–1975)

The fire fighter at the top of the ladder is not fighting a fire, but is only updating the running total of the 1950 Red Feather campaign, the predecessor of the United Way Campaign familiar to most today. This is the Ohio Building, located at the corner of Madison Avenue and Superior Street.

The Fishing Rodeo was popular with children in the 1950s. These events were held at the pond at Pierson Metropark, with prizes for the children who caught the biggest fish.

The George Crosby Real Estate Company was located in this little bit of tyrolean architecture in the early 1950s. Before parking lots became profit makers, Toledo boasted a wide variety of architectural styles. With the need to park cars, however, and increased competition from suburban shopping centers, parking lots began replacing buildings like this one.

The staff of the Stewart Pharmacy, circa 1950. Ella P. Stewart and her husband, William "Doc" Stewart, opened their pharmacy at the corner of City Park Avenue and Indiana Avenue in 1922. They quickly established themselves as leaders of their community. Doc became manager for local jazz pianist Art Tatum, and Mrs. Stewart became active in community affairs and civic groups.

The Toledo Fire Department underwent a reorganization in the 1950s, owing to the new suburbs. Several new fire stations were built, like the new Number 1 Station here at the corner of Huron and Orange streets (which also served as headquarters for the department). Other stations were closed.

Willys-Overland took advantage of Toledo's location as a seaport to ship a large number of Jeep automobiles overseas in the mid-1950s. The company also set up branch production in countries like Australia and Brazil.

Five Points in West Toledo, where Phillips Avenue, Lewis Avenue, Sylvania Avenue, and Martha Street intersect. This photo was probably taken as part of a study in the early 1950s to improve traffic flow in the area, before the construction of the interstate highway system. Lewis Avenue at this time was a route to Ann Arbor.

As shoppers headed to the suburbs, downtown retailers quickly noticed, pressing city officials to attempt to create a "mall" downtown. Both Adams Street and Madison Avenue were closed to traffic between St. Clair Street and Huron Street, and entertainment, gardens, and playground equipment were moved into the streets to create the Pedestrian Mall in 1958 and 1959. The organist here is entertaining listeners on Madison Avenue.

These men are testing the new deep-fording kit for the military jeep, probably around 1955. This test is probably taking place in Maumee Bay, near Point Place. The Jeep has been closely identified with Toledo since World War II.

In an attempt to lure shoppers back downtown from suburban shopping centers, Tiedtke's updated the look of their downtown store, including vanquishing sawdust-laden floors, installing floor tile, and updating the display cases.

In 1953, the Kaiser Motors Corporation bought Willys-Overland Motors, and concentrated on producing only utility vehicles. By 1955, the company was producing only the Jeep and Forward Control trucks like the one in view here. This photograph was taken at the newly opened Toledo Express Airport around 1955.

This 1955 bird's-eye view offers a glimpse of the growth Toledo enjoyed during the first 50 or so years of the twentieth century.

The Toledo Museum of Art has provided countless schoolchildren in the Toledo area with a greater appreciation for art. This school group is visiting the museum in 1962.

These smokestacks are located at the Libbey-Owens-Ford plant in suburban Rossford (ca. 1960).

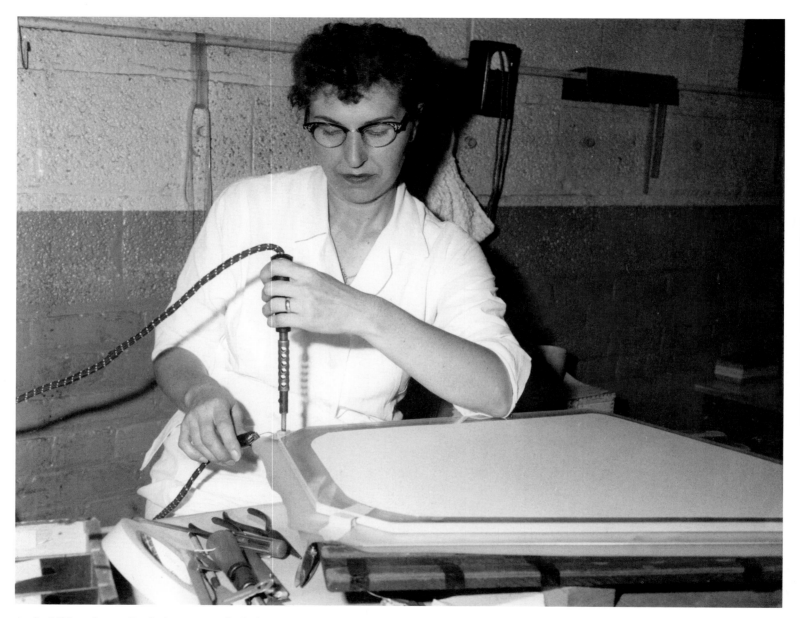

At the Libbey-Owens-Ford plant in Rossford, this woman is attaching electrical components to a windshield to be installed in a jet airplane. LOF also supplied a number of automobile companies with glass components (ca. 1965).

The Columbia Gas Company had this building constructed at the corner of Erie Street and Jefferson Avenue. The building is reminiscent of the work of German architect Ludwig Mies van der Rohe, of "less is more" fame.

Holy Trinity Greek Orthodox Cathedral. Holy Trinity has been an anchor for the near northside of Toledo since its opening. Every large city has a neighborhood that new immigrants move into; North Toledo has served as an entrepot for Germans, Jews, Greeks, Lebanese, Syrians, and others.

Toledo Scale holds an open house for its employees and their families in the spring of 1964. The Toledo scale was another widely known Toledo product. The slogan "No Springs—Honest Weight" called attention to both their design innovation (no springs) and the claim that this innovation prevented cheating (honest weight). The company placed scales in areas where passersby could weigh themselves, which built trust in the product.

From the mid-1960s to the 1980s, the city was being reshaped. One of the anchor projects of this effort was the construction of the new headquarters for Owens-Corning, Fiberglass Tower, named for their most popular product.

The urban renewal projects of the mid-1960s and 1970s greatly changed the appearance of the city. One of the casualties was the Town Hall Burlesque Theater. Rose LaRose, proprietor of the Town Hall, was able to move her business to the Esquire Theater.

Toledoans today mainly look at the Great Lakes as a recreation spot, forgetting that many still make their living on the lakes. In the late fall of 1975, nature reminded those living in the area of just how unforgiving those waters can be. When "the gales of November" claimed the *Edmund Fitzgerald,* they also claimed the lives of seven northwest Ohio residents—including the captain of the ship, Ernest M. McSorely.

NOTES ON THE PHOTOGRAPHS

These notes, listed by page number, attempt to include all aspects known of the photographs. Each of the photographs is identified by the page number, a title or description, photographer and collection, archive, and call or box number when applicable. Although every attempt was made to collect all data, in some cases complete data may have been unavailable due to the age and condition of some of the photographs and records.

29 **City of Toledo Ship**
Toledo-Lucas County
Public Library
a_16920_cityoftoledo

30 **Toledo I Dirigible**
Toledo-Lucas County
Public Library
a_knabenshue_dirigible_190

31 **Conant Street**
Toledo-Lucas County
Public Library
a_13837_maumee

32 **Lawn Fete**
Toledo-Lucas County
Public Library
a_18643_lawn_fete

33 **Boody House Lobby**
Toledo-Lucas County
Public Library
a_boody_house_lobby

34 **National Union Building**
Toledo-Lucas County
Public Library
a_16291_national_union

35 **Nicholas Building**
Toledo-Lucas County
Public Library
a_5772_nicholas_building

36 **Washington Street**
Toledo-Lucas County
Public Library
a_15021_washington_street

37 **Eight-story "Skyscraper"**
Toledo-Lucas County
Public Library
a_13720_star_hardware

38 **Walbridge Park**
Toledo-Lucas County
Public Library
a_12609_walbridge_scenic

39 **Lake Erie Park**
Toledo-Lucas County
Public Library
a_casino_lake_erie_park

40 **Grand Army Decoration**
Toledo-Lucas County
Public Library
a_sub_gar_2

41 **Reunion Decorations**
Toledo-Lucas County
Public Library
a_sub-gar_1

42 **Wamba Festival**
Toledo-Lucas County
Public Library
a_18644_wamba_festival

43 **Madison Avenue**
Toledo-Lucas County
Public Library
a_15166_madison_ave_1915

44 **Great White Hope**
Toledo-Lucas County
Public Library
a_22_dempsey_jamaicakid

45 **Ohio Dairy**
Toledo-Lucas County
Public Library
a_ohio_dairy

46 **Under Construction**
Toledo-Lucas County
Public Library
a_lasalle_construction_191

47 **Willys-Overland**
Toledo-Lucas County
Public Library
a_willys_orchestra

48 **Lucas County Courthouse**
Toledo-Lucas County
Public Library
a_14316_courthouse

49 **Modified Runabout**
Toledo-Lucas County
Public Library
a_13493_edler

50 **Zurfluh Jewelry Store**
Toledo-Lucas County
Public Library
a_16879_zurfluh

51 **Holmes Snowflake Laundry**
Toledo-Lucas County
Public Library
a_snowflake

52 **Circus Parade**
Toledo-Lucas County
Public Library
a_8535_circus

53 **Second National Bank**
Toledo-Lucas County
Public Library
a_second_national_construc

54 **Landing on Water**
Toledo-Lucas County
Public Library
a_5543_airplane

55 **Niagara Replica**
Toledo-Lucas County
Public Library
a_16934_perry_centennial

56 **Perry Centennial**
Toledo-Lucas County
Public Library
a_16931_niagara

57 **Trained Bear**
Toledo-Lucas County
Public Library
a_17093_trained_bear

58 **Scott High School Track Team**
Toledo-Lucas County
Public Library
a_scott_hi_track_1914

59 **Niagara Hotel Fire**
Toledo-Lucas County
Public Library
a_niagara_hotel_fire_steam

60 **Fire Fighters**
Toledo-Lucas County
Public Library
a_trunk_fire

61 **Automobile Display**
Toledo-Lucas County
Public Library
a_sub_grasser_autos

62 **Swing Bridge**
Toledo-Lucas County
Public Library
a_wheeling_bridge_boats

63 **Troops at Ann Arbor Train Station**
Toledo-Lucas County
Public Library
a_doughboys_return

64 **Adams Street**
Toledo-Lucas County
Public Library
a_sub_adams_street

65 **Vita Temple Theater**
Toledo-Lucas County
Public Library
a_10414_vita_temple

66 **Madison Avenue Parade**
Toledo-Lucas County
Public Library
a_knights_of_columbus

67 **Palm Sunday Tornado**
Toledo-Lucas County
Public Library
a_raabs_corners_tornado

68 **Secor Hotel**
Toledo-Lucas County
Public Library
a_lasalles_secor

69 **Niagara Hotel Fire**
Toledo-Lucas County
Public Library
a_niagara_hotel_fire

70 **Boody House**
Toledo-Lucas County
Public Library
a_boody_house

71 **Union Station**
Toledo-Lucas County
Public Library
a_5379_union_station

72 **Central Union Terminal**
Toledo-Lucas County
Public Library
a_2974_union_station

73 **High School Stadium**
Toledo-Lucas County
Public Library
a_scott_hi_football_game

74 **Airport**
Toledo-Lucas County
Public Library
a_8498_adams_superior